Malaya Bronnaya

poems by

Marsha Blitzer

Finishing Line Press
Georgetown, Kentucky

Malaya Bronnaya

Copyright © 2023 by Marsha Blitzer
ISBN 979-8-88838-315-5 First Edition
All rights reserved under International and Pan-American Copyright Conventions. No part of this book may be reproduced in any manner whatsoever without written permission from the publisher, except in the case of brief quotations embodied in critical articles and reviews.

ACKNOWLEDGMENTS

Grateful acknowledgement is made to the editors of the following publications where these poems, reprinted here, some in different form, first appeared:

T*he American Journal of Poetry,* 'Missing the Mark," "Moscow, October 1993"
The Banyan Review, "Moscow 1993," "Conference," "Plummeting"
166 Palms: "Olga Nikolaevna"

I would also like to thank Tina Barr, Greg Wrenn, and Eva Levine for their invaluable guidance and support over the years. I am also very grateful to many friends and family who provided encouragement and critical feedback.

Publisher: Leah Huete de Maines
Editor: Christen Kincaid
Cover Art: Patrick Forte
Author Photo: Charles Blitzer
Cover Design: Elizabeth Maines McCleavy

Order online: www.finishinglinepress.com
also available on amazon.com

Author inquiries and mail orders:
Finishing Line Press
PO Box 1626
Georgetown, Kentucky 40324
USA

Table of Contents

Conference 1

38 Malaya Bronnaya 3

Moscow 1993 4

Plummeting 5

Body Art 6

Missing the Mark 8

Pickpockets 10

Olga Nikolaevna 11

Dacha 12

Necropolei 14

Lev Melikhov 16

Nikolay Solomin, Oil on Canvas, circa 1950 17

The Arbat 18

Thin Skin 19

Pregnancy 20

Sagging 21

Moscow, October 1993 22

On the Periphery 23

Conference

1. The Stalin Years

Mandelstam died in transit. Those who made it
    did hard labor—
        felling stands of pine,
        silver birch, long logs encased
    in white, peeling bark.

They clawed bark, unfurling it to the cambium
    on through into the phloem, shoveled the soft,
moist red into their mouths.
    They swallowed fistfuls of toadstools, milk-
caps, and brittlegills, tore off clumps of moss.
                            If caught, they were shot.

Once spring came sap began to rise—
    birches wept in Siberia.

2. Winter 1995

Giddy foreign investors hopped on the run-down
    Tupolev at Domodedovo to get to the conference
in Novosibirsk. It was only a short haul.
    The flight crew set out folding chairs in the aisles,
squirted disinfectant into the air to mask the aroma
                  of sausage.

When we landed I was escorted to a bulletproof car.
    A corporate lawyer on a rainmaking mission,
I was hunting for naïve businessmen out to make a buck
    in the ex-Soviet Union. I lavished them with vodka
and caviar, assuring them that the Mafiosi wouldn't taint
    their deals. Speaking at the conference I touted capitalism,
a promise of the Wild West. After the last ceremonial meal,
    I went to bed in my coat, baseball bat by my side,
chair wedged at the door.

* * * * * * * * * * * * * * *

There, silver birch has knotty bark, white with black
    streaks, smells of wintergreen. Birch tar is
said to cure stubborn wounds.

In the night, a blistering wind. Willow warblers
    nested, whistling a repetitive, descending dirge.
Snow buntings hid in the grass.

3. Sauna

In the windowless *banya* at a friend's dacha near
    Moscow, we drank straight vodka. Marina's aria
from *Boris Godunov* filtered through a speaker.
    I beat myself with bundles of young birch,
swept myself, as with a broom.
    To cool, I ran outside, rubbed myself in a snowdrift.

Russians say a person is reborn in the *banya*.

38 Malaya Bronnaya

A colony of cats, at least thirty strays, glared
as I entered her flat. Only the stench
of a communal bathroom during the Soviet era
could compete with those uric fumes.

Nelly, the landlady, was once the star aerialist
of the Moscow Circus, lover of director Yuri Nikulin.
He rewarded her with this penthouse on Patriarch's
Pond—home to Bulgakov, Tsvetaeva, Russian *literati*.

Around the pond, odd drunks slept on benches
while babushkas trudged through dirty snow
to give grandchildren fresh air, *svezhiy vozdukh*.

We hired a Swedish firm to gut, remodel
our interior. *Remont*, the Russians call it. With
foreigners coming in droves and a new class
of rich Russians, the word was commonplace.

Our neighbors, Georgian Mafiosi, black market
millionaires, arrived home in limos from the Riviera
and London, wearing designer jeans, the latest
from Harrod's and the Champs Elysees. Mercedes
motorized toy cars for their kids. Upstairs in their
penthouse apartment they ate caviar—"black gold."

Out front, bodyguards patrolled. I saw a machine
gun killing at the kiosk across the street.
A hitman torpedoed one of the neighboring clan.
Rumors of kidnappings circulated amongst expats.
Summer afternoons my son and I ate ice cream, fed the ducks.

Moscow 1993

My tongue melted into wild sturgeon caviar,
large, black pearls—salt, velvet.

I long for the vodka, swallowing fire.

We ate Beluga
from the Georgian market.
It came in glass, the size of
a Skippy peanut butter jar.
We ate it by the spoonful
for breakfast, even my two-year old.

They say a musical ear will hear
the cat's purr of prized
fish eggs rubbing against
each other.

Plummeting

1.
Our rooftops were smothered in snow. Freeze and
    thaw, freeze and thaw.
Through the living room picture window:
    water trickled off the eaves. Tiny pendent drops
grew into shells sheathed in skins of ice. The icicles
    thickened, lengthened downward to dagger point.
Some hung in clusters.
    When one released its grip, crashed, shattered,
the others followed.
    I wished I could glue them back on.

2.
Pedestrians scurried past buildings constructed in the 30's.
    Heat leaked through poor insulation,
melted rooftop snow.
    Menacing shanks of ice soldered together by frost.
On thaw days Muscovites knew to hold something
    above their heads.
One night a three-foot falling icicle impaled our car. My son
    cried. Through his sobs was intelligible the word
Mitsubishi.

Body Art

Broadly speaking, my aesthetician's clientele in Moscow consisted
    of high-end prostitutes. Shy, I turned away when they
slipped out of their clothes for a bikini wax.

"Like gypsies," my husband's grandmother would have said—
    "They don't wear panties!" Her prejudices stretched beyond
the Roma. She would have scowled at the young people who parade
    the Arbat, tattoos snaked around their necks, their foreheads
marked, full-body ink. Not to mention piercings and split tongues.
    Ghoulish photos of Russians who have tattooed their
eyeballs conspicuous on Instagram.

You had to have been imprisoned or a member of a criminal gang
    to have tattoos in the USSR. In the Gulag, they signaled
rank—an intricate caste system, a language.
    Inmates made the ink from burned rubber of boot heels,
mixed with urine, an antiseptic.

I had my lips and eyeliner tattooed with henna when we returned
    to America, brows, too. Cosmetic tattoos were as lucrative
a sideline of my new medi-spa in Potomac as Botox. Twenty years
    on, the dye has faded to a faint pink shadow
on my brows and lips. I hide it with makeup.

My son has a permanent tattoo. As if etched on glass: "8016"—
    the house where he grew up; it is unobtrusive, winks
for just a second when he lifts his right armpit, something he takes
    care never to do in front of his dad.
I never told my parents I converted.

In Tucson, our hair stylist is covered from head to foot.
    She experimented with colored sharpies at age ten,
got inked at fourteen. Now at twenty-six, each drawing
    is a testament to her storied life.

With over twenty tats, she is a collector, flesh, a blank canvas.
    She admires some of her tats more than others. I wonder
if she shouldn't try to cover less favored ones with a layer
    of new ink, a palimpsest.

Her skin is still firm. What will happen as her tattoos begin
    to wrinkle? Or maybe, like the tattooed Toki Doki Barbie
doll, she will never age. I am told this Barbie is popular
    with Russian adolescent girls.

Our stylist, Lena, allows her scribe to inject colored pigment
    under her skin with the pen-like needle. She doesn't flinch,
proud that, unlike others, she doesn't dull her senses with Xanax
    or weed. She wants to feel the piercing.
She has already weathered tattoo flu.
    She is a Bad Ass.

Missing the Mark

On the sawdust floor of the center ring lies the girl with the broken neck.

    Glitter from her tutu scattered on the ground,

        legs flung haphazardly.

Her hand struggled to grasp his, outstretched, just beyond her reach,

    failing.

Her catcher's still hanging, waiting.

I. The Catcher

The Circus on Tsvetnoy Boulevard was girded with heat.

Far above, on a distant bar, the catcher hung
    upside-down, a bat, listening for the girl's sweep.

Rocking his cradle, he had braced himself
    on a swinging steel beam.
He sensed the apparition of her, suspended.

Dizzied, he misjudged her radar—the somersaulting,
tucking and turning, hurtling forward, her wrist for his,
    to fuse in mid-air—

A siren's wail riddled the dome, enough to set us on edge.

II. The Aerialist

She clawed at space, layers of it.
Her descent was slow, then sudden. She plunged.
She has broken into two.
Her legs buckled; her shapely neck and hips, shattered.

III. The Spectators

The ringmaster's bellow, crescendo of a drumroll.
The crowd swallowed, then sucked in air,
Exhaling cheers and whistles.

The crowd is one neck, straining to witness the spectacle,
one cavernous mouth.

Some giggle. The fall, a dark pleasure.

Pickpockets

A cloud of urchins swarmed around the Western-looking
businessman as he walked down Tverskaya Street.
Like a bike of hornets ready to attack, the ravening
kids howled as they circled, before zooming in to
bite and scratch, grab for the wallet in an
unfastened pocket. They were
professionals. Pedestrians scurried
past, so not to hear my
husband's keen as he
swung his arms,
kicked off his
assailants.

Olga Nikolaevna

The way fog fills air around the port in St. Petersburg,
    gradually, Olga's blindness set in.
She expected sacrifice, awaited it. Sentimentality was for Pushkin
    or the new generation.

Moscow is an ugly city, its buildings, dilapidated,
    rat-infested. The smell of urine along corridors built
by Stalin in the thirties, a blessing not to see.

Fuel and food scarce, Olga and her grandson retreated
    to the dacha. The air was fresh, the ground moist.
Olga groped at the dacha's stair rail and along the walls.

The dog was handy, scaring off drunks, left
    an audible trail as he panted, stopping to piss
at tree trunks.

They found open space. Olga sniffed the ground,
    inhaled its narcotic scent;
ground laced through ages with black tears,
    and crouched down on fours,
knees clinging to dirt, palms imploring moss.
    She spread her hands and clawed.
She felt the dog watching.

In pine woods she wanted autumn's best. In better days
    devoured the smooth, soft edible, guzzling vodka.
But when she felt the velvety caps with gills, she froze with fear.
    Steer clear of those death caps—
their potent sweet scent!

Now, crawling, anxious, Olga foraged. Slowly, her basket filled up
    with courage. She tried to pick the good ones.

Her grandson hawks mushrooms at roadside stands.
    Some people have died.
Such rumors she brushes aside.

Dacha

When we sent Mark to pre-school with a fever,
    our nanny Tanya glared—
just as she did when we bought a babushka's mushrooms
    at a roadside stand.

    "She could have been blind,
her mushrooms, poisonous!"
    Tanya took the taste test. Commonsense is relative.

She muttered *Gospodi Pomiluy*—Lord have Mercy!
    at our recklessness.
Summer approaching, she advised us to rent a dacha.
    A cottage would protect our child from
        smog and asthma,
give him more Vitamin D.

A handsome ex-KGB operative drove Mark and
    a nanny, in our Mitsubishi, to a dacha in Yushnove Tushino.
The ruble at an all-time low, my husband said, "This is the only time
    in our lives we'll feel rich." A loaf of bread was pennies.
        There was Luka, the dog, to play with, a room
for napping, a forest with many mushrooms, berries—
    red currants, stone fruit.

My son could identify the safe from the poisonous by age four.
    Tanya, a Russian equivalent of Mary Poppins,
had mysterious powers. As if floating in air, she guided Mark
    through early fog into pine forest,
        talked to squirrels, awakened whole families of
mushrooms. She taught him how to screw out a mushroom
    from the ground. He would squeal at the tiny fungi.

They hunted the edible ones on the trees. Clutched bunches
    of porcini, maslyata, lisichki , with gill tops brown or tan;
they avoided toadstools, death angels.
    When their woven baskets were full, they returned
        home, cleaned their bounty to make bouillon.
Once thrown into the pot, a peeled onion which turned blue
    signaled trouble. Tanya taught my son that.

Necropolei

1.
Yesterday we went burial plot shopping.
There are five left in our synagogue's
section of Evergreen Cemetery.

"Forget stocks, invest in burial plots"
is the mortuary's refrain. So, this is our pick.
We are realists.

Our plot is just off the sidewalk.
There will be pedestrian traffic.
Still, to be fair, Tucson's Audubon Society lists
Evergreen as a bird sanctuary.

2.
When Dad died, my young sons giggled as they gathered
pinecones from evergreens around his grave at
Ascension Cemetery, decorated the fresh, dark soil with
primitive drawings, some cross-shaped. The grownups
left flowers. Jews leave pebbles, heaps of them—odd-
shaped stone structures on top of headstones. Unlike
flowers, stones do not die.

3.
My brother's burial was a family gathering. After hospice,
he went to Irving, the undertaker, who brought him
to Ascension, interred next to his parents.
Like a Russian babushka, our matriarch, Cousin Kathy,
trims the grass around the headstones of our relatives, buried
nearby, children of early Polish immigrants.
I wish I could give her a bench to sit on; it's hard work.
Some of the tombstones were sinking, as if in quicksand.

4.
In Moscow in the 70's, I stood in line for five hours to view
Vladimir Lenin's preserved corpse in a glass case
at Red Square. Whether it was turning green was a topic
of hushed debate among locals who threaded their way.

Today, like pilgrims who visit the relics of Orthodox saints
in Russian monasteries, foreign tourists flock to the mausoleum
after months of Covid. Die-hard Communists lay carnations
at Vladimir Ilyich Ulyanov's feet.

5.
Large, sculpted monuments, small chapels. Novodevichye
Cemetery is an open-air museum. The graveyard boasts
one of the world's most impressive collection of corpses,
the resting places of luminaries, Anton Chekhov, Nikita
Khrushchev, Boris Yeltsin, Mikhail Bulgakov, and Dmitri
Shostakovich.

6.
It was my twenty-first birthday, when I took the train
to Peredelkino. Boris Pasternak is buried near three pines.
Iron fences surround the graves. Russians know to close the door
of the fence when leaving a grave to contain the spirit
of the deceased.
Cellophane wrapped roses lay on Pasternak. Muscovites
carried newspaper-wrapped volumes, his poetry,
left behind a shot of vodka.

Lev Melikhov

His studio in the Museum of Folk Art, off Sadovoye Koltso
    seemed as large as the rugby field we lived across
from in an English village years later.
    The physique of a boxer—beefy, burley—he wore
an unpruned mustache and thick whiskers.
While the impression was ferocious, sweat would cling
and twitch on those hairs when he smiled, curl up with delight
    in the presence of my toddler, who would kiss him smack
on the lips. Ticklish to a two-year old.
    Under his beret, one eyebrow cocked upward more
than the other. Suspicion was his vocation.

Almost thirty years ago we sat for a portrait. Black and white.
    Light and shade.
Like a rare bird, I preened, struck a pose and smiled.
    Lev intervened, advised that a smile could be interpreted
as a sign of insanity or dim-wittedness.
    Solemn, I looked Russian, almost. I lost my nationality
under his eye.

Age has faded one portrait. We appear as ghosts of ourselves.
    Mark sits on a chair looking up,
as if towards the supernatural. We stand beside him,
    looking downwards, as into a well.
The man behind the expat family is Lev.

Nikolay Solomin, Oil on Canvas, circa 1950

I step back from where it hangs, monumental, in our Tucson home
    to enter into his representation: a *kolkhoz*, Stalin's legacy.
We outbid a French law firm to acquire it back in Moscow
    in the early 90's.

I walk along into a Russian village and into the collective farm.
    It is the Soviet era—the potato pickers are rosy-cheeked,
muscular. Students, workers, the 25,000'ers, have come to assist
    villagers during the harvest—their sacrifice to make real
Lenin's promise: "Peace, Land, Bread." A classless society.
    They relax on carts driven by draft horses. Blue skies,
green grass, a combine harvester—socialist realism at its best.

In the end, failure to work on a farm, meet quotas, meant
    hard labor or worse. Naïve idealism gone sour.
In the 70's, we rich kids fancied ourselves budding communists.
    To aid the cause of my brigade, I even stored a cache of
weapons under my dorm room bed. In Westchester County
    revolution was sexy.
The older sister of my high school friend, a few years earlier,
    plastered posters on her wall of Chairman Mao.
You had to enter her room through a beaded curtain.

The Arbat

The Arbat was already tacky then.
I thought I bought a garnet necklace from an antique dealer
– twenty years later an insurance appraiser
in Washington, DC told me it was fake—colored glass beads.
But still I made more reputable purchases—
the Hilary Clinton nesting doll, I have it still.

It was pure chance that two Stanford grads
would meet on that cobblestone street, each pushing
strollers, one wearing a sweatshirt broadcasting university
allegiance. And further that they would start a nursery
for expat kids in an apartment leased by Reuters
on Sadovoye Koltso. Journalists—primarily, British,
Americans, Japanese. We held Board meetings.

On winter mornings our toddlers would arrive
with their nannies to learn to dance and sing Russian songs
led by Masha, their Russian teacher. We attended performances
to observe their development. The teacher told me that
Noah and Mark were leaders. I was flattered, I had underestimated
my son.

Thin Skin

A predisposition for happiness
can't be bought,
not even for a million rubles.
Take it from me—
Thin skin, pampered, protected, and
crafted over millennia,
unlike escargot, securely ensconced
in their shells.
I had always used a harpoon
to impale snails from the Caspian Sea
on my starter plate at the
Hotel National off Red Square.
In America, I am starting to grasp them
with an ordinary tong, waiting
for a creature to emerge.
I can envisage a pearl, too.
But I surreptitiously wrap
shell and would-be pearl
in a paper napkin before the waiter
takes the plate away.
Dissipated, the illusion.

Pregnancy

The migraines were intense when I was pregnant. Nauseous,
　　　pain pierced through my temples. I crawled into
our Mitsubishi before twilight, hubby at the wheel.
　　　Destination: The American Medical Center.
I was a frequent guest. Its personalized service in Moscow
　　　in the 90's cherished, coveted as much as concierge
medicine nowadays in the West.

Lying in the back, I envisaged our route, had it memorized.
　　　We left the parking lot behind our building on Patriarch's Pond,
turned right on Ulitsa Malaya Bronnaya, and took another right turn
　　　onto Sadovoye Koltso. Periodically my husband had to stop
for me to vomit on a curb, always by the time we reached the U-turn
　　　at the Peking Hotel. Just another right onto Ulitsa Krasina,
before finally turning right onto Ulitsa Yuliusa Fuchika—the AMC!

The morphine was a black-market purchase from the Russian
　　　ambulance attendants, the safest treatment for a pregnant
woman and fetus. Eric was born months later.
　　　I surrendered to oblivion like a drug-addicted child of the
Russian middle class.

Sagging

It shows on my face, my eyes. I tilt my head back-
    wards when I drive, hold an eyelid
up with one hand when I write.

Drooping was gradual. Skin slid down, from
    my brows over my eyelids to meet my lashes,
threatening to obscure my pupils.

Two decades ago, my lids were plump and pretty.
    We lived in Moscow, as experts from the West.

In my prime, seven months pregnant, I saw the ice dam
    break. I had watched the sitting room ceiling sag
beneath autumn's ice.

At first, a large damp patch. Then sludge crept in. Melting
    snow dripped through the roof of our flat
on Malaya Bronnaya.

Large clumps of wet plaster kept falling into the gang of
    buckets and pots borrowed from the kitchen, the bath.
Tanya, Lucya, and Katya laid towels on our parquet floor.
    They were PhD's from Lomonosov Moscow State University,
grateful for work in the new Russian economy.

Once the ice had thawed a company fixed the roof,
    but it bowed, leaked again.
Our landlady told us we should have shoveled.
    I never saw people do that in North Chicago.

When the elevator jammed at the sixth floor
    I waited for it to plunge.
I shouted help (*pomogi*) in Russian. Our neighbors,
    the Gocha brothers, pried open the doors.
Russian men are so good at that.

Moscow, October 1993

Spectators craned forward to see the fleet of gigantic
green goliaths file down the main drag, Tverskaya.
Army tanks loaded with democracy.

We stayed safe indoors to watch CNN. Airborne troops
and tanks shelled Parliament, the *Byely Dom*.
Giddy, we made champagne toasts to President Yeltsin
and the reformers: our friends and colleagues. Opposition
to free market reform and a return to communism thwarted.

Snipers haunted rooftops; they were flitting shadows.
One almost killed the American paralegal balanced
on a window ledge. She wanted to have a better view
of the civil war. He shot her in the kidney.
As a souvenir, some friends saved her bloody jacket.

On the Periphery

Soon after storing their furs:
    sudden sweltering heat—
snarled-up streets—thick smog.

We flee the megalopolis,
    navigate our Mitsubishi through mud,
around potholes. My stunt driver husband coasts over
    each undulation.

Once safe on the outskirts, we garden, pickle,
    parade nude
in a log house adorned with carved platbands, not a
    McMansion, *kottedzh* of the
new rich. Our dog Luka snoozes while Mark learns to ride
    a bike, swim, and fish.

I learn how to tend the samovar,
    Charlie, the *shashlik*—
he marinates mutton and skewers it over wood
    from the nearby apple orchard.
We grow cucumbers and strawberries,
    medicinal plants on our plot of land.

Middle-aged dachniks, we carry out repairs: hand-sewn curtains,
    a new shower, greenhouse—ongoing *remont*.
We like to pretend we are Russians.
    Wearing fur hats in winter, we can do
a fair imitation. But who can teach us
    to play the balalaika?

Down the road behind a gate live some former
        astronauts of the USSR—
    They lend glamor to our existence.
          Yet today we will have fish soup,
ukha, for lunch. Trout from the nearby stream makes
    a thick broth, a shot of vodka lends a bitter taste.

Marsha Blitzer is a poet living in Tucson, Arizona. She was born to Polish American parents and grew up in North Chicago, Illinois where her father was superintendent of schools. She is an alumna of Sarah Lawrence College (B.A. in Russian), completed the coursework for a Ph.D. in Russian Literature and Linguistics from Georgetown University, received a degree in law from Suffolk University Law School, and an M.S. in Education with a specialization in creative writing from George Washington University. As an attorney, she specialized in international antitrust and corporate law at the Federal Trade Commission in Washington. In 1991 she moved with her husband and young son to Moscow where she lived for four years practicing corporate law at Baker & McKenzie. After moving to London, where she lived for almost eight years, she devoted most of her time to raising her two young sons and teaching Russian law at the University of Surrey. Her poems have appeared in The American Journal of Poetry, Atlanta Review, The Banyan Review, Cleaver Magazine, The Moth, Persimmon Tree, 166 Palms, and elsewhere.

She notes that the Russia she lived in during the 1990s was a period of hope for the country's social and political modernization. The present period in Russia is very different.

www.ingramcontent.com/pod-product-compliance
Lightning Source LLC
Chambersburg PA
CBHW022129090426
42743CB00008B/1062